<u>The Forgotten</u>… This Book is about the many people who live on the streets, the many people who are suffering from depression, substance abuse, domestic violence, child endangerment, and much more.

<u>The Forgotten…</u>Attempts to make aware that we are all GOD's people, we all should not be forgotten and we all need help at some time in our lives…

Thanks be to GOD for HIS purpose and to HIM be all the Honor and Glory…Now and Forever. Amen.

This Book is dedicated to DLMW, DDW, JAW…

Special acknowledgement to Denise Evans who helped tirelessly with instructing and assisting with this Book.

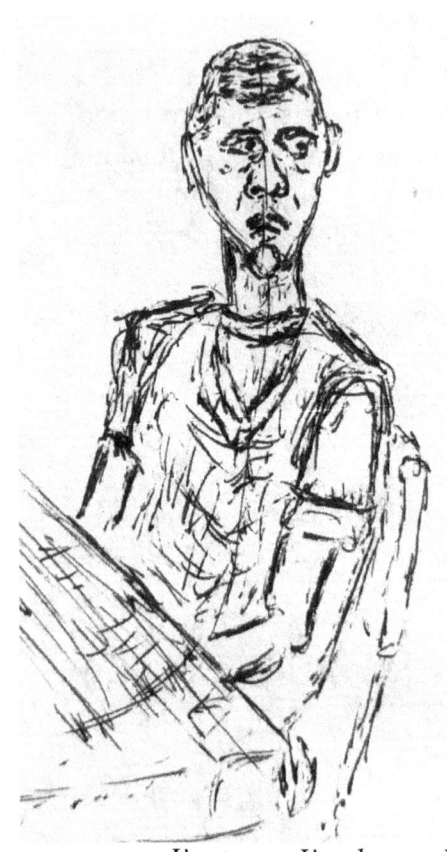

I'm torn…I'm down…I'm Hungry…I'm Homeless…Please Help…Don't Forget Me…

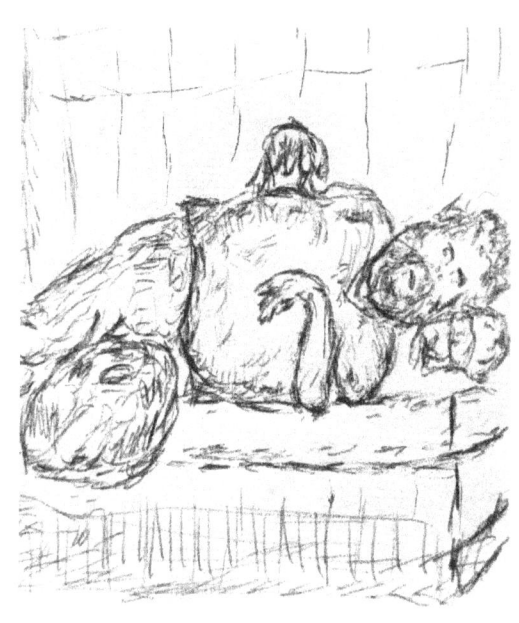

Sleeping in this alley...raining...cold...hard concrete...sirens wailing...bugs crawling...People walking by... Don't Forget Me....

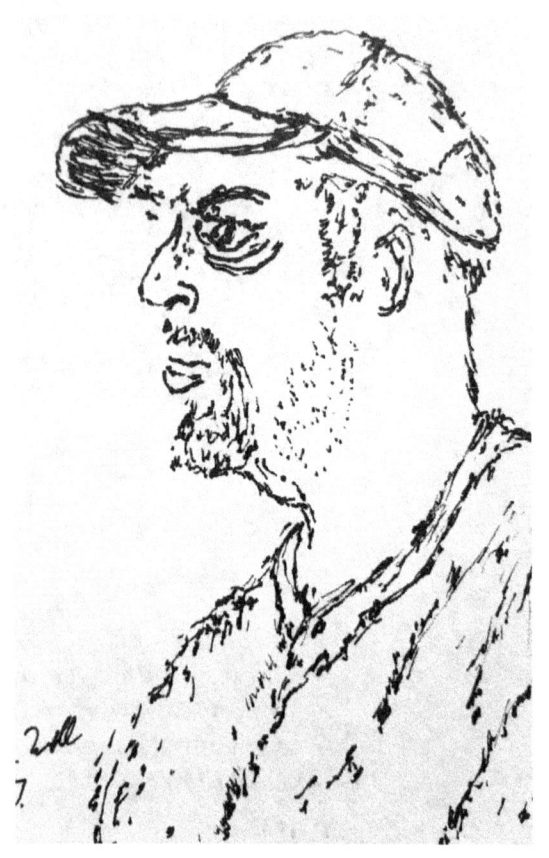

Please Don't Forget Me… I'm tired…I'm Hungry…

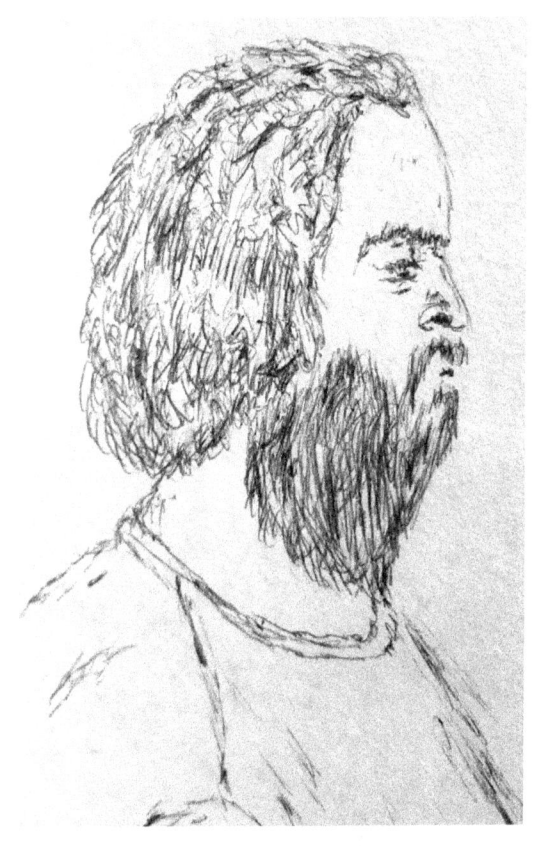

What?...Who is that talking in my head?... What?...Who?... Its' two people... Mental Health affects us all in some way... Don't forget me...

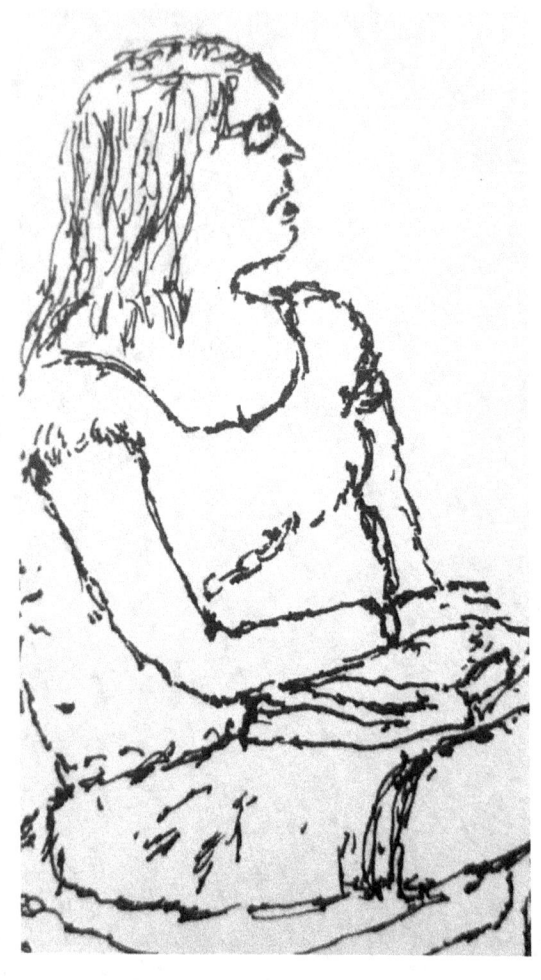

I'm scared...I'm trying to hold it in...I'm running from him...Help Me...Don't forget me...Domestic Violence is prevalent and needs to STOP...

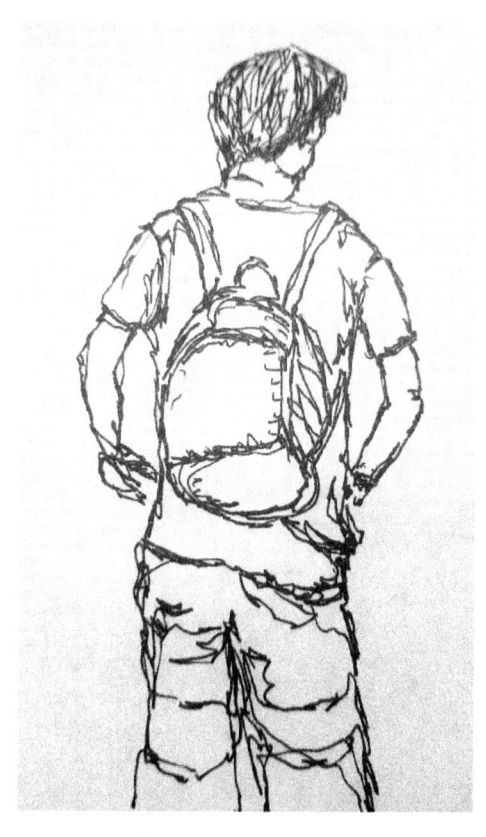

All I have is what is in this backpack…One shirt…One pair of pants…Don't Forget Me…

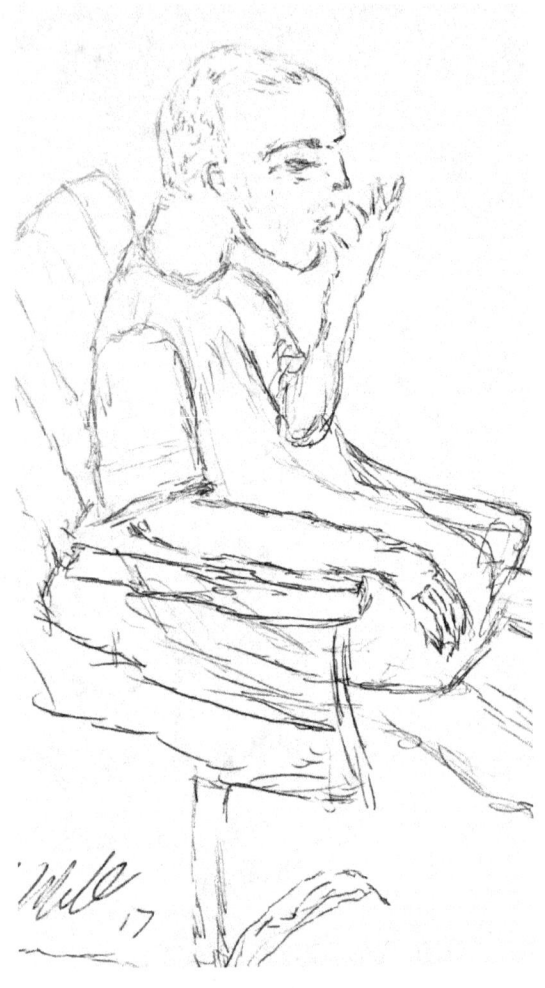

Child homelessness...Is Prevalent...Has no boundaries or age limits...No Child should go hungry...Don't Forget Me...

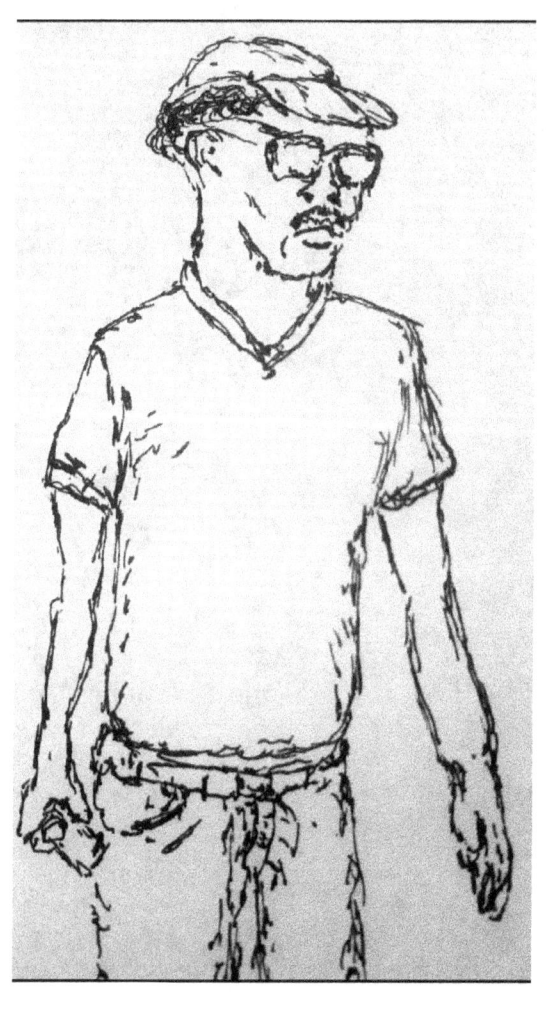

Don't Forget Me...I can't See...But I can Hope... I can feel... I can hurt... I can believe... Don't Forget Me...

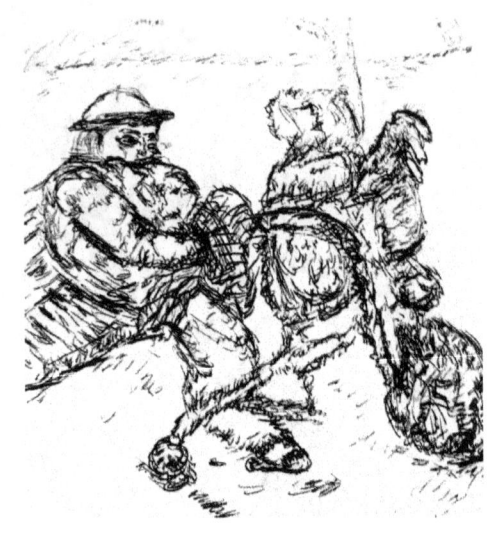

Bags...Bags...Please Help Me...I'm covered in these Bags...all of my belongings...in Bags...I'm Becoming my Bags...Don't Forget Me...

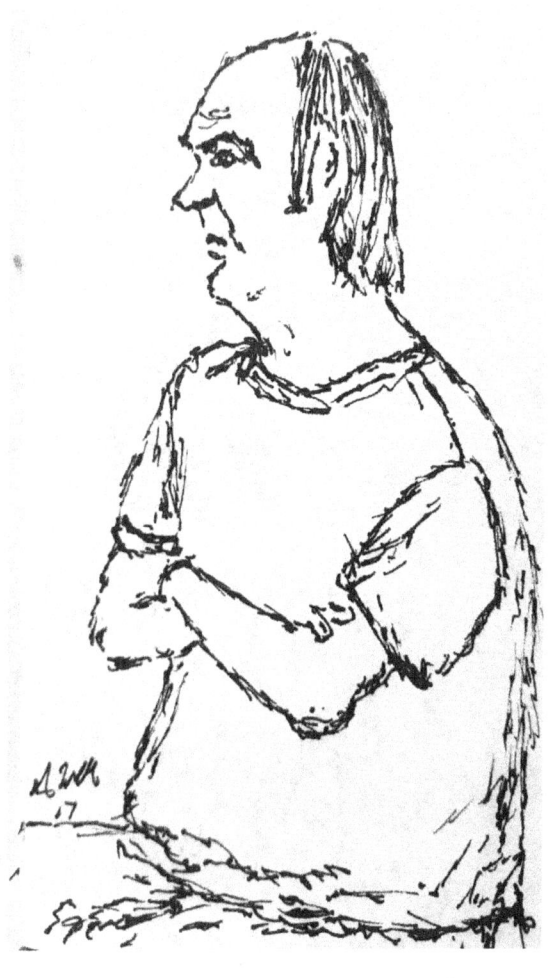

*Don't Forget Me...I'm not lazy...
I will work...But I have no
support...I have no family...I
need Help...That's all...Help.*

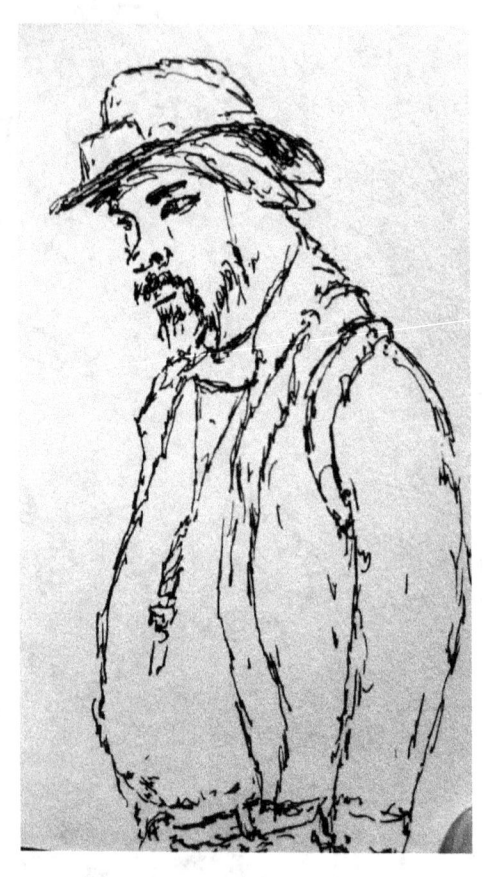

I am SOMEBODY...Don't Forget Me...

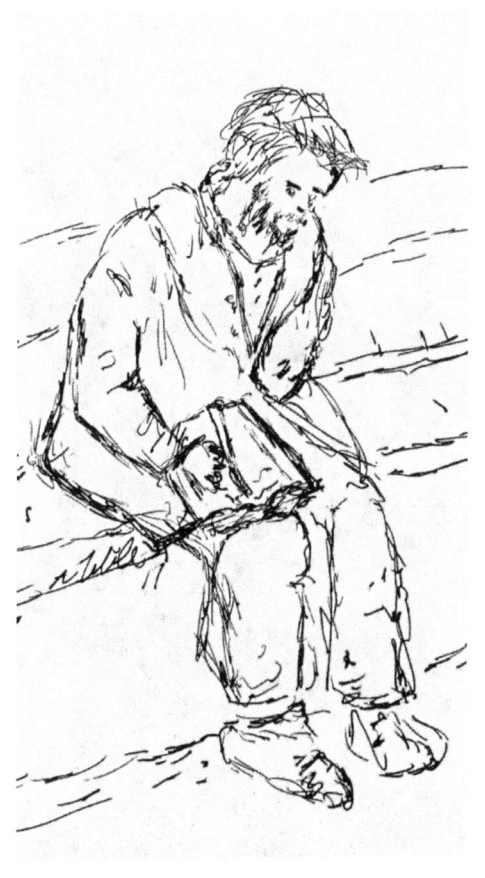

Don't Forget Me...I'm sitting here...I'm cold...I'm writing...But I'm COLD... I'm Educated...But I fell on Hard times...Help me...

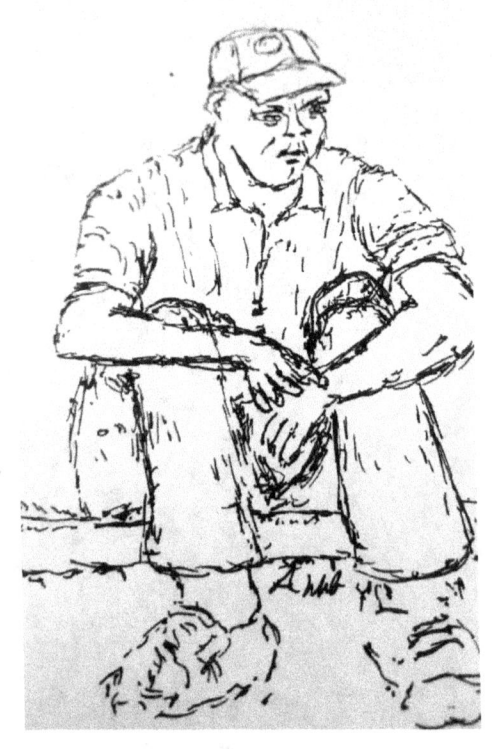

People Judge Me...Because I live on the street...People Don't know me...they don't know my struggles...Just talk to me...Don't Forget Me...

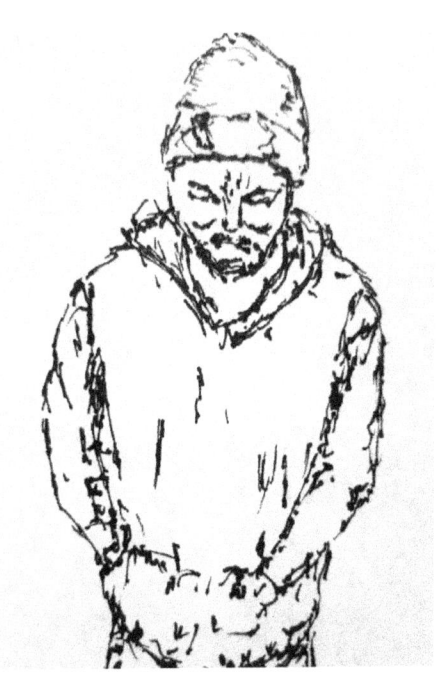

I'm Forgotten...no one cares...They don't know that I still exist...They don't care that I still exist...Please Just help me...and...Don't Forget Me...

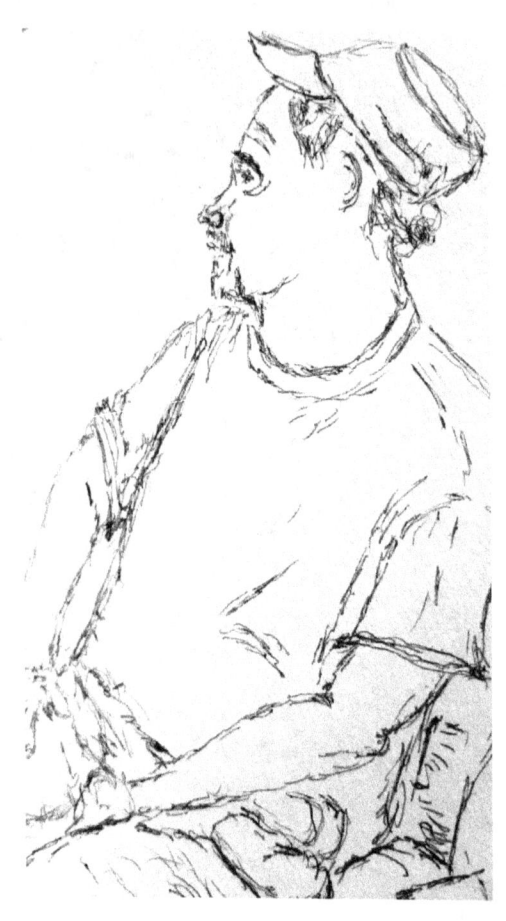

Many of us are talented...Many of us have dreams and goals...we are not lazy... Don't Forget Us...

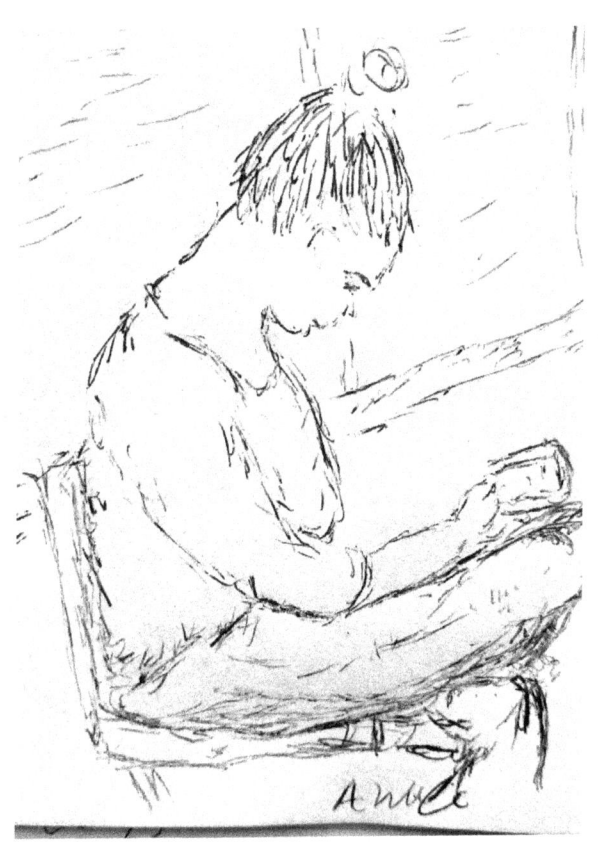

Why does he not love me?...Why do I sit here waiting on his call?...Why did he put me on the streets...? Don't Forget Me...

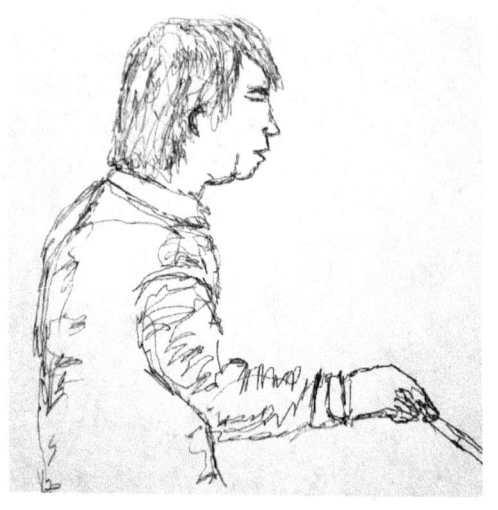

I can orchestrate...I have many talents...Please Just give me a chance... I may be different...I may be Blind...But I can achieve...Don't Forget Me...

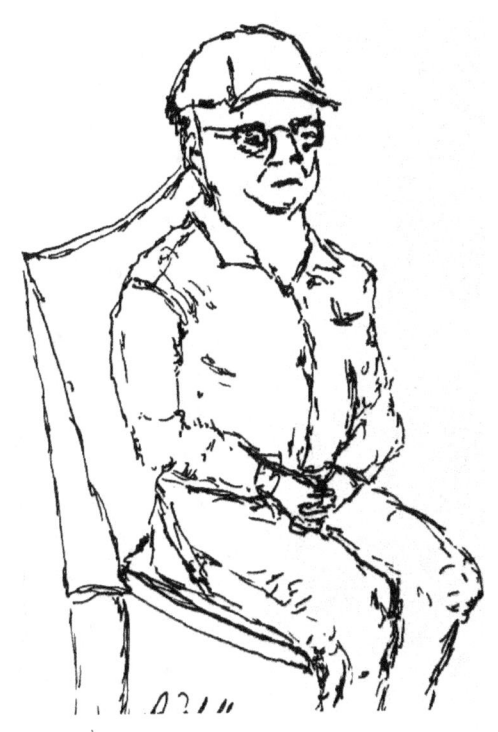

Sitting here...Sitting here...Just Sitting here...I don't know what happened...I don't know why I got here...Everybody has forgotten me...Everybody...Please...Don't Forget Me..

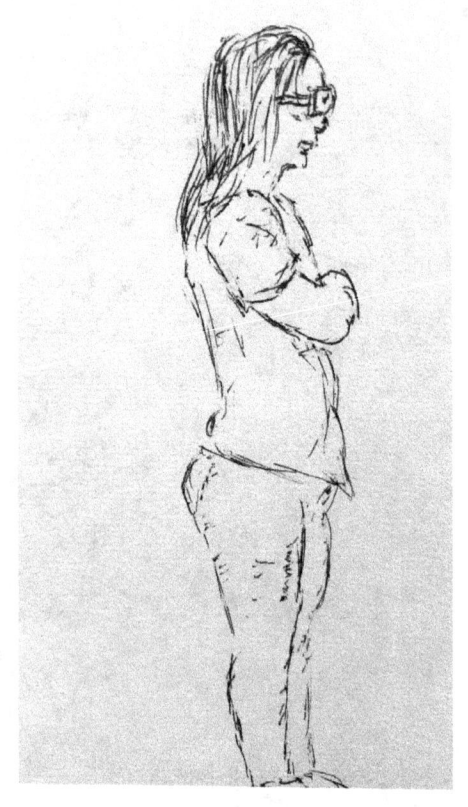

I'm standing here...waiting for something to eat...I'm starving...I can't think...I'm HUNGRY...Don't Forget me...

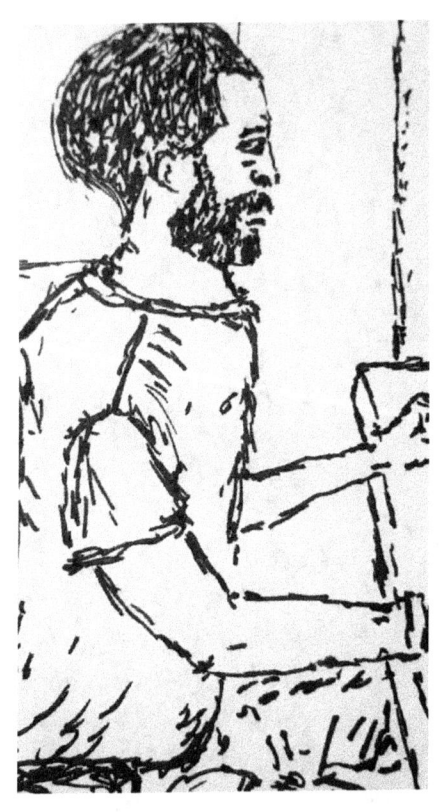

Looking for work...I can't read, but I will work; I don't have a great education, but I will work...I may not be the best for the job...but I will give my best...I will give my all...Just give me a chance... Don't forget me...

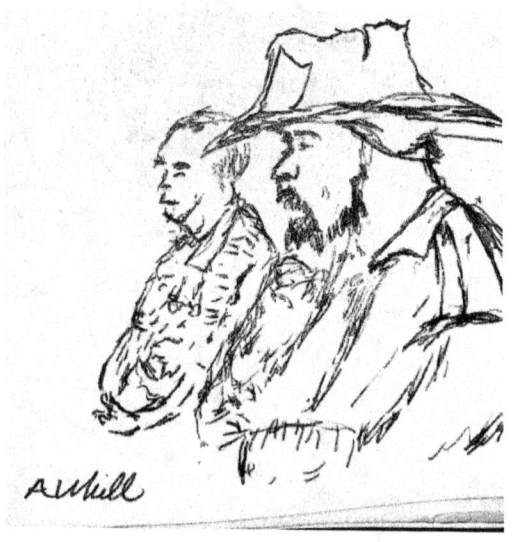

Friends...Us two...In this place...We struggle as friends...We strive as friends...

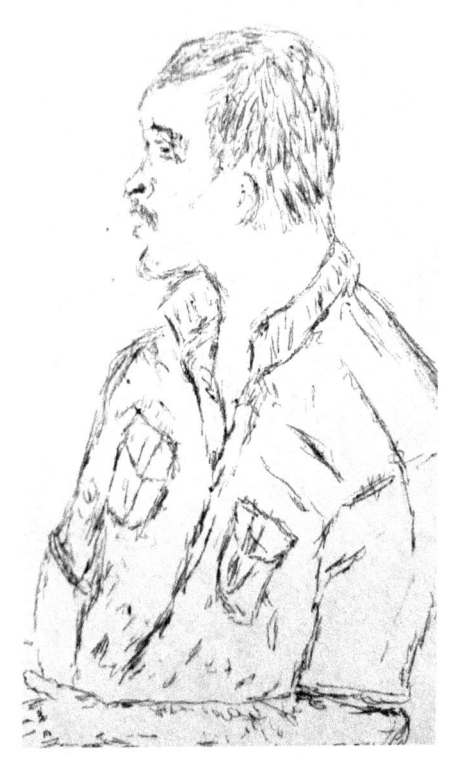

I won't give up...I won't give in... I will keep striving...I will keep praying...I will keep hoping...

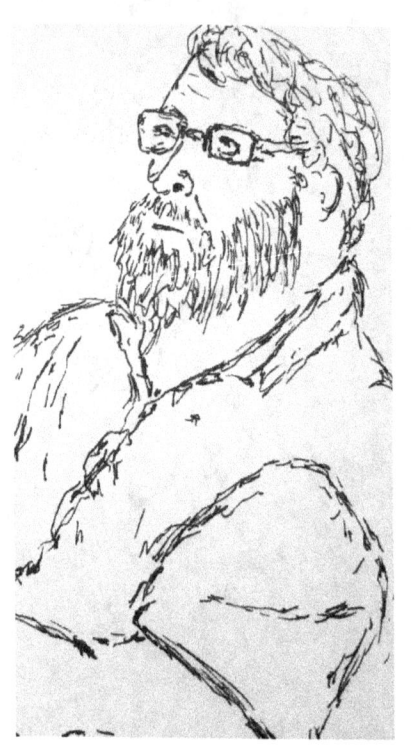

I may not have a home, but I have Hope...I may not have a job, but I have Hope... I won't be forgotten...I will continue to push forward...

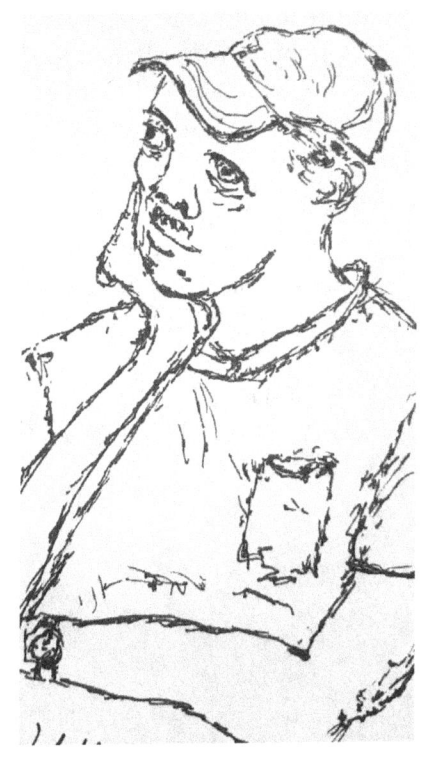

I sit here...I think...and I think...I still serve a wonderful GOD...no matter my condition...GOD will provide...GOD will not forget me...I hope you won't forget me either..."the least of these"... (soon to come).

About the Author:

Anthony Wills is an Urban Sketch Artist and Illustrator…He attempts to sketch and draw people from life and to show how we all ARE and can BE placed in very vulnerable and difficult situations in our life…

Wills will attempts to bring Awareness to many Vulnerable Populations through a series of books to come…

MAY GOD CONTINUE TO BLESS YOU ALL, AND THANK YOU FOR YOUR SUPPORT…

Ant Will

www.ingramcontent.com/pod-product-compliance
Lightning Source LLC
Chambersburg PA
CBHW050038230526
45470CB00003B/1335